THE POWER OF OPTIMISM

BY ABBY COLICH

BLUE OWL
BOOKS

TIPS FOR CAREGIVERS

Social and emotional learning (SEL) helps children manage emotions, create and achieve goals, maintain relationships, learn how to feel empathy, and make good decisions. The SEL approach will help children establish positive habits in communication, cooperation, and decision-making. By incorporating SEL in early reading, children will be better equipped to build confidence and foster positive peer networks.

BEFORE READING

Talk to the reader about what it means to be optimistic.

Discuss: Name a time you were optimistic about something. How did you know you were feeling optimistic?

AFTER READING

Talk to the reader about why it is important to stay optimistic.

Discuss: What is one benefit of optimism?

SEL GOAL

Children may have a difficult time understanding the benefits of optimism and why they should practice it. Explain to children that certain mindsets, or ways of thinking about things, can trigger reactions in the brain. These reactions can affect how they feel in their mind and body. Being optimistic can help them feel good both mentally and physically.

TABLE OF CONTENTS

CHAPTER 1

WHAT IS OPTIMISM?

Charley works hard on her school project. She has a lot of work to do. But Charley believes she will finish on time and get a good grade. This makes her feel happy while she works on the project.

Charley is optimistic. Optimism is the hope that things will go your way. It is also about seeing the good in things. Optimism is a mindset, or a way of thinking.

CHAPTER 2

BENEFITS OF OPTIMISM

Being optimistic has many **benefits** for your mind. It can lessen **anxiety** and **depression**. Optimistic people are happier. They are more **resilient**. Ava fell on her bike. But she got back up and kept riding!

Shane's family is moving to a new town. Shane is hopeful he will like his new school and make new friends. His optimism helps him feel less anxious about the move.

Optimism starts in the brain. Scientists found that optimistic people have a larger orbitofrontal cortex. This part of the brain helps you make decisions. It also helps you feel **rewarded**.

orbitofrontal cortex

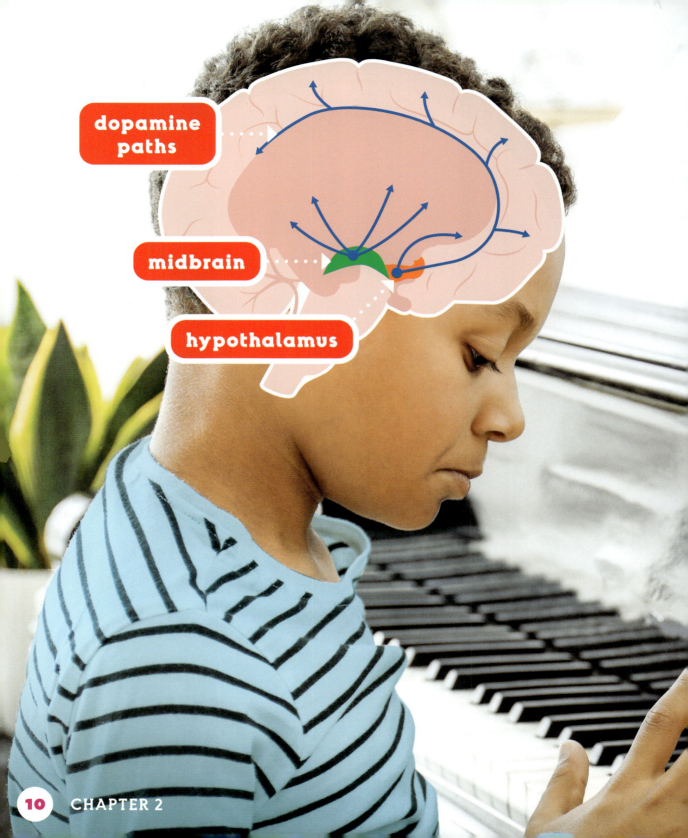

dopamine paths

midbrain

hypothalamus

Being optimistic can help your brain make more dopamine. Dopamine is a **neurotransmitter**. It is made in parts of the midbrain and the hypothalamus. It helps **motivate** you. It also helps you feel **satisfied**.

Carter has a piano recital in a few days. He is optimistic he will do well. This makes him feel good. It helps motivate him to practice.

Scientists also studied the bodies of people who are optimistic. They found that optimistic people have healthier hearts. They get sick less often. They sleep better.

PESSIMISM

Pessimism is the opposite of optimism. It is the belief that things will not go your way. Pessimism can have negative effects. Pessimistic people may experience more depression. They may also get sick more often or not sleep well.

CHAPTER 3

HOW TO BE OPTIMISTIC

Are you optimistic? Everyone can be. But it may take some practice.

One way to be more optimistic is to focus on the good. Ray broke his arm. He has to miss the entire baseball season. Instead of thinking about what he is missing, he focuses on what he can do. Ray decides to take a drawing class instead.

Practicing **gratitude** can help you see what is good around you. Think about or write down what you are thankful for.

Kate is thankful for time with her grandma. Thinking about what she is grateful for helps her see what is good in her life. This helps her be more optimistic.

If something does not go your way, think of a time it did. Remembering times that went well will help you be more optimistic.

Hans didn't get the part of the school play he wanted. He was disappointed, but he is thankful to be in the play. He does his best to practice his part.

KEEP IT REAL

It is possible to believe a good thing will happen even if it is not likely to. This can lead to disappointment. You can prevent this by being **realistic**. If you are trying out for a team, you may feel optimistic that you will make it. But you need to accept there is a chance you may not.

Optimism has many benefits. Seeing what is good around you can help you be more positive and feel happy. How can you practice optimism?

TOXIC POSITIVITY

Toxic positivity is pressure to only focus on the positive. When something bad happens, it is OK to feel upset. Pushing away your feelings when you're upset can hurt your mental health. Instead, tell yourself, "It's OK to feel upset. When I'm ready, I'll move forward."

GOALS AND TOOLS

GROW WITH GOALS

Being optimistic has many benefits. Seeing the positive in your life can help you be more optimistic.

Goal: Each day, write down three good things that happened to you. Focusing on good things can help you be more optimistic.

Goal: Practice gratitude. Write down the people and experiences you are grateful for. Practicing gratitude can help you be more optimistic.

Goal: When you are facing something hard, remind yourself of good things that can happen. Repeat good outcomes to yourself, such as "If I study, I will pass my test."

TRY THIS!

Journaling is a great way to help you sort through your feelings. Write about an event you have coming up. Write down everything that can go badly. This can help you feel prepared and remember to be realistic. Then, write down everything that could go well. Try to focus on being optimistic that the good things will happen.

GLOSSARY

anxiety
A feeling of worry or fear.

benefits
Things that produce good or helpful results or effects or that promote well-being.

depression
A medical condition in which you feel unhappy, irritated, or hopeless, can't concentrate or sleep well, and aren't interested in activities you normally enjoy.

gratitude
The practice of showing appreciation or giving thanks.

motivate
To encourage someone to do something.

neurotransmitter
A chemical messenger in the body that sends information from one neuron to another.

realistic
Seeing things as they really are.

resilient
Able to adjust to change easily.

rewarded
Feeling satisfied or encouraged.

satisfied
Pleased because you have achieved something.

TO LEARN MORE

FACT SURFER

Finding more information is as easy as 1, 2, 3.

1. Go to www.factsurfer.com

2. Enter "**thepowerofoptimism**" into the search box.

3. Choose your book to see a list of websites.

INDEX

Blue Owl Books are published by Jump!, 5357 Penn Avenue South, Minneapolis, MN 55419, www.jumplibrary.com

Copyright © 2024 Jump! International copyright reserved in all countries. No part of this book may be reproduced in any form without written permission from the publisher.

Library of Congress Cataloging-in-Publication Data

Names: Colich, Abby, author.
Title: The power of optimism / by Abby Colich.
Description: Minneapolis, MN: Jump!, Inc., 2024.
Series: The power of positivity | Includes index.
Audience: Ages 7–10
Identifiers: LCCN 2023033251 (print)
LCCN 2023033252 (ebook)
ISBN 9798889966951 (hardcover)
ISBN 9798889966968 (paperback)
ISBN 9798889966975 (ebook)
Subjects: LCSH: Optimism–Juvenile literature.
Classification: LCC BF698.35.O57 C65 2024 (print)
LCC BF698.35.O57 (ebook)
DDC 149/.5–dc23/eng/20230801
LC record available at https://lccn.loc.gov/2023033251
LC ebook record available at https://lccn.loc.gov/2023033252

Editor: Katie Chanez
Designer: Emma Almgren-Bersie
Content Consultant: Megan Kraemer, MSW, LICSW

Photo Credits: PeopleImages.com - Yuri A/Shutterstock, cover; South House Studio/Shutterstock, 1; michaeljung/Shutterstock, 3; DaniloAndjus/iStock, 4, 5; triloks/iStock, 6; travelism/iStock, 7; Prostock-studio/Shutterstock, 8–9 (foreground); Tachjang/Shutterstock, 8–9 (background); Pixel-Shot/Shutterstock, 10–11; bluedog studio/Shutterstock, 12–13; Nurhudayanti/Shutterstock, 14; jayfish/Alamy, 15 (foreground); Circle Creative Studio/iStock, 15 (background); mixetto/iStock, 16–17; Jupiterimages/Getty, 18–19; hanapon1002/iStock, 20–21.

Printed in the United States of America at Corporate Graphics in North Mankato, Minnesota.